The Place Where Memories Grow

Phoenix Grace

Presentation by *BookLeaf Publishing*

Web: www.bookleafpub.com

E-mail: info@bookleafpub.com

ISBN: 9789358316704

First edition 2023

DEDICATION

To all those who've weathered life's storms, found strength in faith, and discovered the eternal beauty of growth, "The Place Where Memories Grow" is lovingly dedicated to you. May these words serve as a testament to the resilience of the human spirit (strengthened by God), and an enduring reminder that, like the verdant forest, we too can thrive in every season of our lives

ACKNOWLEDGEMENT

This collection would not have been possible without the unwavering support and encouragement of so many. My deepest gratitude goes to my family, whose love and patience sustain me every day. To my mentors, friends, and church family who offer new ways of seeing, believing in (but not of) the world. To all the women of Arise with Grace, who have trusted me with their stories of pain to promise and who have , in turn, empowered me to take a leap of faith of my own. To my readers, for whom I write with an open heart, and to God, who lights my way on this poetic journey. Thank you for being a part of "The Place Where Memories Grow."

PREFACE

In "The Place Where Memories Grow," you are invited to embark on a profound journey of faith, self-discovery, and transformation. These verses are a testament to the resilience of the human spirit, the healing power of faith, and the enduring beauty of life's many seasons. Phoenix Grace takes you through the depths of despair to the heights of inspiration, embracing life's ever-changing landscape. As you delve into these pages, may you find a sanctuary of words and a testament to the enduring strength of the spirit.

In my dreams, I sometimes go

In my dreams, I sometimes go,
to the Place Where Memories Grow

Laughter, tears,
through all the years
Root themselves in fertile ground

Dear God,

Dear God,

Everything I said (say)
And everything I did (do)

Has been about striving,
searching

Looking for me,
And looking for You

I seek to experience my life unfolding

I seek to experience my life
unfolding
Ripe with possibilities-
the fruit plump
and golden

The withered vines, the lands untamed
are a part of self-
not hidden and shamed

It is all beautiful,
honoured,
and named

From spark to seed,
To sapling and tree
It is all part of me

Leafy splendour

Leafy splendour- full and rich
nourished dreams that have come to pass

Memories deep- rooted in dark soil
Without sunlight and proper care
Stand in stark contrast
       With leaves stripped bare

In the Borderlands

In the Borderlands

Between Here
and there,
Now,
      and
            Then

Betwixt
      and
            Between
Is an Uncertain
Place
       to be

Behind you is
    a story

Before you is
    His Glory

The middle is a riddle.
    a mountain,
       a mystery,

You pray for hope,
       an answer,
              a rope,

Then, in the wind,
       a whisper says,

          Now is the time to-
              Learn from the past
                  Live in the present
                     Look to the
                        future

In the Borderlands
is where you are meant to be

Shrinking inside herself

7

 Shrinking inside
herself
to protect
the middle,
the fragile core

Heart turns to stone-
  feel no pain

Fossilized joy
  Is buried deep

Stumbling around IN THE DARK

I was stumbling
    around
        IN THE DARK
Flailing about
    with my
        arms
    wide open
      clinging,
        grasping

Searching for a
      WAY
 OUT

When, I heard a
    voice say,

"You see with your heart,
      and hear with your soul"

Then, a path opened up
 in front of
    me

and, step

        by

step

I was lead

    INTO

        THE LIGHT

Kaleidoscope

I am broken, fragmented

Inside out,
>   upside down,
>   turning around
and around
>   No clear picture of who I am

Microcosm
Macrocosm

Chasm of the soul
>   No clear purpose

>   Then- ILLUMINATION

Beauty seen in the eye of the beholder

"Beloved," He calls me

I was CREATED
>   In the image of the one who
made me

I am no longer broken-

IN HIM

I am

       Whole and Holy

              Unique

Chosen

            A Child of God

Daughter of the King of Kings

Made by God to stand up and stand out

I was made by God to stand up
and stand out

Not sit down,
shut up
be shut out,
or shut down

repressed,
suppressed,
oppressed

Not give in
under stress
or
duress-

made to feel
less
than
         the rest

I am not who people say I am
My identity is not of man

I am a Child of God
We are all Children of God-

Sisters in Christ

We can choose to make it right

Not gossip and fight
(Be ruled by might)

We are all here together
We can love one another,
support one another,
encourage one another

Be the Light
Be the change
we wish
to see

No matter the crime,
We are redeemed by Christ

He is the judge,
not you and me

Tender seedlings

Tender seedlings,
Newly planted
Not one thought or experience
Taken for granted
Living presently, in the moment
Full of potential
Waiting to happen

Wordless Wood

I walked into the wordless wood
filled with anger, pain
and grief

I met a willow who wept for me
And embraced me
with His branchy
Leaf

There I found myself- quite beyond belief
Filled with calm, grace and peace

Whole and Holy
Oh, sweet relief!

Windows and Mirrors

I sit inside on my sunny sill,
and watch the world
go willy nil

Outside, i think,
it is dark, not bright
Full of strife, and ruled
by might

I much prefer my inner calm
To wheel a balm
Rather than
Wield a bomb

I relax in thinking the truth,
so clear

When, suddenly,
In Spirit's voice, I hear:

Remember, dear one, each of us
Is a mirror for the other

You see the world not as it is,
But as you are

You are both dark,
and bright,
Calm, and strife
Inner, and outer,
Human, and divine

Each one no better than the other

Take my hand and follow me.
It is about the journey,
AND the destination
The key is not to do, but to be

As you look in more deeply,
You will see out more clearly

The Word is both a mirror and a window

Somewhere betwixt and between

Somewhere
betwixt
and between,

lies the bridge
       between
Sacred
and
Obscene

I dwell in
the gaps,

In meager
and mean

And wait for the
"I Am"
to be
Heard
 and
Be
 Seen

At the end of yourself

At the end of yourself
        you find the way

Stretched out
and up

and beyond your limits
Unsure,
        Uncertain
Not knowing where you are at
        or where you are going
You reach out
        You reach up
You have faith
        You step out
You find your wings
and you fly…

Spread Your Wings

Have you ever felt like the brilliant butterfly-
Emerging from its chrysalis,
Expecting to soar past the horizon,
to lands unconquered.
and dreams not realized-
only to be trapped in the filmy nothingness
of reality?

If so, remember,
You too have the butterfly's
brightly colored hues-
Talent,
    Ability,
        Resilience
And the strong wings capable
of taking you
  Beyond   sky
     the   the
      furthest   of
        reaches

Fragments of Grace

Scattered shards
>of broken down rock

reflecting

>>Light from Above

Warmth
>rising,

Cool turquoise
>>beauty-
lapping

>>>in pools
Fronds
>of foliage

in vibrant hues
>of growth-

The smell
>of hope
>>and freedom

Arise with Grace!

As dawn's first light breaks through the night,
A rebirth in faith, a sacred sight,
I leave the past, embrace God's plan,
A new creation, by His hand.

In Christ, I find the strength to soar,
Letting go of what's gone before,
Transformed by grace, I stand in awe,
In His love, I'm born once more.

In trials and storms

23

In trials and storms, I'll stand my ground,
With faith as my anchor, strength is found.
Though dark clouds gather, I won't despair,
In every hardship, I'll find hope's flare.

With courage in my heart, I'll face the night,
Through adversity, I'll seek the light.
Resilient spirit, unwavering soul,
In life's challenges, I'm made whole.

In Shadow's Deep

In shadows deep, my soul did wane,
Lost in doubt, consumed by pain.
But faith emerged, a guiding star,
Redemption's promise, near and far.

Through grace and mercy, love's embrace,
I found in faith a sacred place.
From darkness to the light I'd tread,
Redeemed and whole, my spirit led.

Lord of my life

I love you Jesus,
you are
Lord of my
life

I give you all of me,
In the midst of all
this strife

Use this broken vessel
to help heal
a broken world

Trials by fire,
transformed by faith
to gold

Anger, pain, and grief-
finding no relief
Pushed to the margins,
held captive by sin

I call upon your name,
hoping to reclaim
all the promises

You did proclaim

Now,
your peace
Is in my heart
Sign of a new start

Use this broken vessel
to help heal
a broken world

Trials by fire,
transformed by faith
to gold

The Place Where Memories Grow

In my dreams, I sometimes go,
to the Place Where Memories Grow

Laughter, tears,
 through all the years
Root themselves in fertile ground

Oh, verdant forest, evergreen
Tell me who I am and where i've been

Leafy splendour- full and rich
nourished dreams that have come to pass

Memories deep- rooted in dark soil
Without sunlight and proper care
Stand in stark contrast
        With leaves stripped bare

Oh, verdant forest, evergreen
Tell me who I am and where i've been

Tender seedlings,
Newly planted

Not one thought or experience
Taken for granted
Living presently, in the moment
Full of potential
Waiting to happen

Oh, verdant forest, evergreen
Tell me who I am and where i've been

I see the future of this wood-

Mixed growth forest
Strong and free

Full of life giving birth to life
Working together
From spark
To seed

                              to sapling
To tree
Bearing fruit of love and peace

I see the willow and the pine
The apple and the birch
The cedar and the maple too
And in the centre,
Standing together- the mighty oak
And the lilac intertwine!

Oh verdant forest, evergreen,
I now know who I am and where I've been

And I am planting seeds
Of the future
Yet unseen